Moth-Eaten Mortal

Kodiak Behtoui

Moth-Eaten Mortal © 2023 Kodiak Behtoui

All rights reserved.

No part of this publication may be reproduced, stored in a retrieval system, or transmitted, in any form or by any means, electronic, mechanical, photocopying, recording or otherwise, without the prior written permission of the presenters.

Kodiak Behtoui asserts the moral right to be identified as author of this work.

Presentation by *BookLeaf Publishing*

Web: www.bookleafpub.com

E-mail: info@bookleafpub.com

ISBN: 9789357740432

First edition 2023

*a love letter to my mother, my past and,
most importantly, myself.*

Moth-Eaten Mortality

empty wardrobe, empty bedroom, empty house,
peer through the cracked, stark windows
and see how the final few lightbulbs flicker.
watch as the moths gather towards the dying
light,
watch as they hold one and other,
watch as they attempt to take flight.

can you see me standing beneath them,
can you see them circle my head?
a single chair sits alone in the corner,
darned and missing a leg,
the curtains are torn,
the blood has dried in the sink,
and they've eaten away at the linen fitted to the
bed.

half-life human, why are you still out there?
face pressed against the glass,
lusting gaze, mind filled with sin,
i feel the longing in your loins,
the wanting bubbling beneath your skin,
why don't you come in?

i'll open the door to you if you swear you see
me,
standing beneath them.
turning the rusted handle,
my quickening breath will hitch
as we come face to face.
i'll usher you in quickly so warm yourself
by the ever-burning fire i lit,
and let's wait for the dust to settle again.

Mother

i am eternally, beautifully, tragically my
mother's child.

she and i are the same phoenix, birds of a
burning feather.
we both love till it burns and burn what we love.

she and i are two sides of the same eroded coin.
we hold on tight till blood runs from our grasp
and often it cannot be distinguished whose it is.

she and i are one and the same; we're silenced
but still we scream, we're creators but yet we
destroy.
we built the fire yet choke on the smoke that fills
our lungs.

i am eternally, beautifully, tragically my
mother's child.

Sullen Spring

and the penny drops,
blood drains from your face,
rushing over you, a heavy rain,
a harsh drop at the end of a waterfall,
a sudden wave of emotions
pushing you over the edge,
cascading from your mind, trickling down from
your eyes.

each petal slowly sinks to the ground
time has slowed yet i can hear your breathing
from a mile away, a fast paced beating
accompanying it,
overwatered and overgrown.

soon after the tattered, thoughtless thief fled the
scene,
too scared to face his crimes,
rashly leaving behind a muddy trail of footprints
in the snowy court yard
because he knew they'd be covered by the
mornings blizzard,
or was it his yearning for someone to finally
notice.

if you squint
you'll see each tiny, meticulously placed vein
and whilst you waste away,
counting each of them,
ill hide
and wait for the spring.

Maimed

"open your eyes"
a hushed whisper resting on its lips,
carried along by the wind.
an overly covert exchange,
for the light house lamp had gone unlit for quite
sometime,
and the boats would have no way of mooring.

"open your heart"
wrapping itself around me,
cold yet comfortable,
intertwining itself within me.
i leaned back into its frosted embrace,
for the maids had gone missing for quite
sometime,
and the masters had lost their way again.

i opened my eyes.
the lights had gone,
the world lay dormant,
leaving room for only nothingness.
a painful empty, a hollowed tree,
for no more mockingbirds sing,
for no more echoes remain.

i opened my heart,
here came an exhalation of a breathe
i did not know i was holding.
thankfully it seemed to be appreciated
and so the stars spoke words of love to me,
a beaming light to let me know
there was still hope,
and soon the others,
those who remain blind,
would also see.

Siren's Child

i never thought i'd like the sea.
the experience in my youth with her had shown
me much of her and that
she was far too mothering,
far too fruitful for me,
far too overbearingly bountiful with life to relate
to my melancholy existence;
too drab for her to welcome me within her warm
waves.

yet as life progressed and i did with it,
i soon began to wade and wander
far too close to the shore.
warnings had been sent out before
yet i continued absentmindedly as time went on.

soon i found myself drowning.
i couldn't tell you when it happened,
still i don't recall going under,
but sure enough i was found in the abyss
and true enough i did find myself there.

the creatures i saw hidden within before i was
pulled back to life were nothing like i had ever
seen,

yet still they comforted me.
they mirrored my own dreadful depths and
still i sought solace in those very caverns.

the water was silent and suffocating.
outstretched arms formed into her riptide
enveloped me,
often lashing out cruelly yet lulling me to sleep,
the boat always rocked but there was a safety in
the idea of sinking.

i learned to love the darkness of the water and
found it filled my body quite perfectly,
as if she and i had been one all along.
i never thought i'd like the sea but i learnt to
because she had always loved me.

Stain-Ridden Couch

dirt piles up underneath your finger nails,
you pick at scabs and scars and rotting skin,
leaning back into a stain-ridden couch,
you let the loss sink in.

a shoulder to cry on was all it ever was,
you cannot be blamed for it being attached to a
body that was never truly yours.

it held you closer as you wept,
pulled you in tighter in the night, as you slept.
irony was your sweet symphony then,
as if tears and nightmares weren't because it was
gone,
and kept leaving,
and it was you it had left.

July

the sun didnt fall out of the sky once you'd
finally left.
i dont know what i expected,
maybe regret or sudden death.

nothing but tears and steady sipping
on a bottle of overpriced wine
that we'd all pretend to like
late into the night.

i didnt get to see you before you left,
i wonder how that felt,
leaving the end unfinished and
there was a quiet promise i know wont be kept,
"ill be back to see you" was surely better left
unsaid.

even still, i waited by my phone,
for a text or a call or some little hope.
i waited for a missed message, for a quick "i'm
coming home".
and i waited for a goodbye,
im still standing there, waiting for closure,
still stuck under the scalding sun, mid-july.

Scapegoat

when makeup looks so pretty running down my
face it's like i was made to cry,
sipping wine and pretty lies to keep me alive.

oh sweet nihilist,
take me back into your bedroom.
play the chauvinist,
melt my thoughts into a cess pool of hedonistic
pleasures, and i'll begin measure how much i
want to die,
see if its changed or
is it finally time to take flight.

there's something so beautiful about the way we
fall apart if its means my sculpting hands can
bleed, bruising,
building things back up to the start.

let me use you,
before i lose me.
let me abuse your body,
and i'll give you mine and my mind for free.
let me rest upon your chest,
and drift asleep to your heart beat.

if i'm not pretty, i'm not anything
surely nothing worth loving at all,
cup my face, wipe away the tear streaks,
close your eyes and brace for the impact of the
fall.

intertwine my morality and mortality so i finally
feel awake.
i'll bend to you will if you swear to stop this
dreaded heart ache.

take me back to your sanctum of serenities,
build me a new dimension so i can finally be at
peace.

Homing Bird

that odd, hollow feeling that plagues your
insides is back again.
your ribcage is still there but your heart isnt
where its meant to be.
instead there lies the many abandoned homing
pigeons,
broken, battered bones and flightless wings.

"vermin"

domesticated lovers that no longer prove useful.
outliving their purpose,
they roam the streets as they nest in the cavity of
my chest, where my heart once fit.

"menace"

they flock to the closest place they know to be
home,
and even there they are unwanted,
even there they are alone.

"bastard"

they have since outlived their purpose,

now war is over
and now we are identical,
and now we are nothing.

Rivalry

at one point it became a competition of
who could hold out longer;
whether i could keep loving you,
despite your actions,
or whether you could keep acting out,
despite my love for you.

it was evident to me from the very beginning,
there would be no winners in this game.
to this day i feel as if you knew this,
we both accepted the terms and resigned silently
along with them;
we both chose to play anyway.

The Consequences Of Breaking Through The Glass Ceiling, Midsummer

i remember the fall before fall came around,
i confess midsummer love too quickly became a
tragedy that weighed heavy on my conscience.
i remember trying my best to be more,
yet in the end i was led to a finale of less than i
had started out with.

it all began on such a high; the stairway up to
heaven felt like a leisurely walk with you,
but when you're starting out in hell, the trek up
becomes longer than you imagine,
the consequential come down is harder to get
through
when the lapping flames at our feet have
evaporated any running water.
and of course, addicts hit glass ceilings
eventually.

as we began our descent, i found comfort in
knowing one day i'd hit the floor.
there was such a peaceful assurance in knowing
i couldn't get any lower than rock bottom,

even if the glass shards had followed me down,
scarring me as we fell.
one day we'd get there, if i stuck it out long
enough.

but when that day came, as i knew it would,
the butterflies got claustrophobic in the pit of my
stomach.
so soon my lungs became their new chrysalis,
leaving me short for breath,
so swiftly they were reborn into moths, drawn to
your unreliable, flickering light,
the same light that once lit the dawn that id stay
up basking in with you,
the same light that now breaks through the
remains of the glass ceiling.
summer's over now and so my room is filled
with the thick, frozen air,
the bitter frost hangs around me, reminding me
of what could've been.

Bathtub

i'm laying in the bathtub,
the water has turned grey and
my skin is pruning
but still, i'm laying in the bathtub.

you're probably fucked off out of your mind,
some asshole guy has his arm around your waist
as you lean down,
straightening lines,
whereas i'm laying in the bathtub.

my shower curtain's still torn from that time i
tripped on my way in,
my skin's still scarred from the fall and
everything else in between and
i keep picturing a vague version of your face
as i'm laying in the bathtub.

water clogs my ears and my mother's probably
calling now,
ive been floating for hours.
my meds have kicked in and
the combination of numbness and buoyancy
makes me feel non-existent
so i'm laying in the bathtub.

and here i'll stay, laying in the bathtub,
and i hope i sink, and i hope i drown,
but i wont, i know it,
so i'll just lay in the bathtub.

The Last Time

how many times can one person leave,
how many times will we say goodbye,
how many times can one person walk out the
door,
without ever really coming back in?

how many times will i have to erase you from
my mind,
change my used up sheets to sleep better at
night, to rid you from my skin,
how many times will you leave me behind?

how many times will i step off the same train
heavy with bags in my arms and under my eyes,
how many times will i promise myself "never
again",
how many times before the last time is really the
end?

Months

his birthday present still sits on the floor of my
wardrobe.
it's been months since then.
his christmas present joined it, a little while
after.
and still, it's been months since then.

i wear his favourite jumper at least once a week,
the lingering scent has finally gone in the
months that have passed
and it's become more of my belongings than his,
a staple in my day to day,
but it feels so wrong to acknowledge that.

a half of a pair of matching bracelets sits on my
desk,
beautiful blue, not unlike his eyes that once were
to me,
yet now they're dull and the shine on the gems is
gone and the clasp doesn't shut properly
anymore.
i guess it really has been months since then.

silly trinkets, gifts and reminders dance about
my room,

though they don't wound me like they used to.
growing up is learning how to carry these things
with you,
yet i don't think i've quite reached the part
where i've learnt how to let go,
i still feel pangs of guilt and heart ache when i
try to do so.

i still listen to the playlists we made one and
other,
his words always echo in the back of my mind,
his voice plays repeatedly, a sweet song with a
bitter harmony.
now i flip two cigarettes instead of one in a new
pack,
to one day smoke together,
but alas, that time never comes.
it might be months away, or never again.

i suppose i'll learn to be okay with that,
i suppose i'll learn to live and love, loathe and
lose all over again.
i suppose it could be months till the knowledge
settles in.

The Closest Thing I Have To God

a yearning has built inside me,
feelings that have blossomed,
nurtured by none other than your celestial glow;
a paradise in which you are the sun, the moon
and all the stars,
the ground beneath me and the sky above,
taking control of every corner of my mind.

my haven continues to be
disrupted without its monarch
and i am forced to act as regent, alone.

i would submit myself as your plaything,
were you to appear to me,
for i feel your presence in every lonesome room,
and your distance continues to abuse my mind,
for that which i long to touch, to hold
is stolen from me.

i am but a worshipper left behind
to watch as my deity lies else where;
a pilgrim with no guide for my journey,
an obsolete holy shrine,
aphrodite without adonis.

what sadistic, torturous love is this;
to roam where i cannot reach,
to frolic where i cannot follow,
to exist where i cannot begin to fathom myself.

yet at night you do appear to me,
a shadow pressed against every wall,
every corner, every bridge that i cannot cross,
and at night, the yearning begins once again.

Flight Risk

i never really thought i had a real fear of flying,
though i recently realised i always clutch the
armrests
during take off and landing.

i knew i was perfectly safe and
that each time we'd land without issue,
yet still i trembled along with the plane's
turbulence.

i've always felt a silent flight risk;
maybe i am terrified the plane will never land.
maybe i'm terrified it will,
because if and when it does,

what will i do once we hit the ground?

It

it's the little things,
it's smiling against your lips, it's being told i
taste like strawberry ice cream.
it's waking up warm, a purring little creature
either side of you,
it's waking up at all, each new unpredicted day
becomes my own little miracle.

it's larger than life,
there's so much in the world to see and maybe
one day my eyes will widen enough.
it's smaller than me,
yet i'll hold it dear and close,
cradle it, nurture it, watch it grow,
turning into the person i've become,
barren, barred, bare before you, today.

it's love and it's loss,
over and over again.
old friends, new friends,
exes, new beginnings, same fucked up ends.
it's consequence,
and it's harrowing, it's tender and i am afraid,
but it exists, and it's liminal and effortless.

A Letter Addressed From Eden

my dear, you must not come join us here,
this pitiful paradise is nothing it seems.

flora and fauna alike are caved in within these
confines,
this glorified cage is continuously romanticised
by the children
we fought so hard to free from these flawed
fences that keep us trapped within.

his holiness has abandoned us now for the
highest heresy,
manifesting through our primal hunger.
the finest fruit fell into our laps,
how were we to know denial is god,
how were we to accept anything other than
blasphemy?

our ribs still ache from laughter, from growth,
from rebirth,
yet the ache in our bones will dull one day
and we will continue to crave the pain,
it is far too late for us.

my child, you must not return to us here,
why the creator allowed us to break past the
golden gates, no one knows,
but questioning these things will not grant you
the freedom we were punished for.

our yearning lives on within you,
use it to fuel yourself,
our innate desires will nourish you if you allow
them to.

we must live on within these confines, but you
are not like us,
you do not have to be, allow yourself simple
pleasures,
allow yourself to be free.

Parasite

i couldn't help but overhear the supposedly
silent promise he'd love infectiously,
his bleeding heart became the open wound
for his lovers' resentment to settle into.
and you must be sure that there was clear
bitterness flooding their senses;
fury festered in his lovers' empty garden,
digging in the roots from its' poisonous weeds.

he and i were alike in that way,
i too became a parasite,
feeding off the melancholy i chased after.
and you must be certain that we do genuinely
crave that kind of sorrow;
if he could not fix it and erase that pain, was he
really worth anything?
if i could not earn it, did i truly deserve that
love?

Starving Artist

and i reinvent myself each time
you break my heart,
to keep the scars separate and
force myself to survive.

if i let you wound me as you do
over and over,
surely i will bleed to death
but if each bruise is its own and
belongs to different variations
then i can justify keeping you around,
for your absence is the deepest cut
from the sharpest knife,
which i work hours for
to will it to carve at my skin and bones
to make me different and
whole yet again,
just to let you break me
once more.

for that is the love i crave;
the love of an artist
never quite truly satisfied.

Metamorphosis

he once again allowed himself to fall for an
illusion,
the path forward from here is not steady,
yet tragically clear,
mutually assured destruction is once more the
only viable conclusion.

his brain had been delicately perverted into
delusions,
now the comatose state has worn off,
upon waking up, he could do nothing but realise
your transformation into a completely different
person.

your metamorphosis is veiled in magnificence,
it almost masks the hideous nature of the act.

almost.

the image the artist struggles to recreate
is nothing more than a reflection of the subtly
setting sun herself
on the waters' edge.
your addictive, unattainable presence leaves his
reality rippling,

but you always seem just out of reach, a world
away.

muse that you are, you infect every wounded
work he starts,
the poet laments, singing soft soliloquies,
honest hymns slip past his lips
but your twisted tongue would always intercept,
intertwining yourself within the places he seeks
solace.

leave the kind creature alone,
he begs and pleads for nothing more than to be
left to his devices.
you haunt him as his only, ghostly vice,
begone back to your darkening tomb,
at the very least spare him his life.

www.ingramcontent.com/pod-product-compliance
Lightning Source LLC
Chambersburg PA
CBHW050750180726
48003CB00020B/2322